WRITERS REPUBLIC

A Mirror Into My Soul

ALEXIS WHITE THOMAS

This publication contains the opinions and ideas of its author. It is intended to provide helpful and informative material on the subjects addressed in the publication. The author and publisher specifically disclaim all responsibility for any liability, loss, or risk, personal or otherwise, which is incurred as a consequence, directly or indirectly, of the use and application of any of the contents of this book.

WRITERS REPUBLIC L.L.C.
515 Summit Ave. Unit R1
Union City, NJ 07087, USA

Website: *www.writersrepublic.com*
Hotline: *1-877-656-6838*
Email: *info@writersrepublic.com*

Ordering Information:
Quantity sales. Special discounts are available on quantity purchases by corporations, associations, and others. For details, contact the publisher at the address above.

Library of Congress Control Number:		2021931555
ISBN-13:	978-1-63728-146-8	[Paperback Edition]
	978-1-63728-091-1	[Digital Edition]

Rev. date: 01/18/2021

CONTENTS

Episode Two
The Many Faces OF Love

Episode Three
Suffering and Pain

Episode Four
All About God

Episode Five
Happy Birthday...Happy Times,

Episode Six
Miscellaneous

DEDICATION

This book of poetry truly looks into the depths of my soul, it is lovingly dedicated to anyone who's heart has been broken, felt untold joy, pain and sorrow. A special dedication to my niece Lolita Smith Braxton.

To all who know and understand that the struggle is real

ACKNOWLEDGEMENT

I would like to thank God for the ability to put my feelings into words.

To my family who believes in my ability to put it on paper. My daughters, Stephanie Lawson and Latosha Kessell, my beautiful and talented granddaughters Alexis Huff and Lauren Kessell, my amazing grandsons Ian Lawson and Kai Kessell, lets not forget my super intelligent great granddaughter Britain Rane, my handsome great grandsons Ian Lawson Jr. And Giovanni Lawson, finally my loving husband Ricky Thomas.

My prayer is that each person who reads this book will experience joy, sadness, hope, pain and a revitalization of life. "Go on, take a look into my soul".

Alexis White Thomas
aalexispthom@gmail.com

SADNESS

The sadness that I feel inside,
Sometimes it's more than I can take.
Sometimes I want to run and hide,
As my heart breaks.
A mirror, a reflection, a trace of a smile,
Sadness, fear and desperation simply nothing worthwhile.
Frustrations bound by limitations, is there no way out?
My soul feels only humiliation, I have nothing to shout about.
I hang my head, for my heart won't let me believe,
With each day I am disappointed, there is just no need.

MY LIFE

I'm mixed up and confused,
Lord, what am I supposed to do?
I don't feel as if I belong,
Just a wandering soul, a long way from home.

My heart is heavy I'm just so sad,
No one cares and that kind of makes me mad.
My life has no purpose, I am so tired,
Wish that I could run away and hide.

Did I live all these years to feel like this?
I am not alive I only exist.
From sunup to sundown, nothing in between,
My heart is broken and it's not a dream

The wind is blowing, the sky is blue,
I'm lost and alone, Lord even with you. My life is disappearing
before my eyes, can someone tell me why I'm not surprised?

WHY CAN'T YOU TREAT ME FAIR

I was born black is that a crime.
Why do I have to be cheated all the time?
Why can't you just treat me fair?
God created me with loving care.
Why do you want me to live second class?
Why do you think that I can only wash your dishes and mow your grass?
I bleed red blood, I hurt and cry just like you,
So why don't you want me to have a good life too?
I pay more for everything that I get,
It's so unfair for my paycheck is less.
I work, I work until the close of day,
That's why I can't understand why you treat me this way.
I'm both intelligent and smart, yet, you make my way so hard. Pitfalls
and obstacles you put in my way, know for sure that I am here to stay.
Why do you treat me so unfair, I think it's because you really don't care?

A Message To The Young

Hello young boys and girls, you are the future
leaders of this world. Study hard and stay in school,
remember that it's better to be smart than cool.
Success is not a magic portion; it comes by hard work
and devotion. Don't let the streets lead you astray,
give your life to Christ and always pray.
With education, you stand a chance, you can be anything that
you want, even President of this land. Set your goals and set them
high, someday you will reach them if you really, really try.
Each minor achievement let that be your reward, for a slow
beginning can be a great start. Keep a smile on your face, a
prayer on your lips and a book in your hands. Someday before
you know it, you will be that successful woman or man.

BLACK DOES MATTER

Hands up, I can't breathe,
Please don't knock me on my knees.
All this nonsense has to stop,
Not another brother needs to be killed by a cop.
Black really does matter,
Need to cut out some of this senseless chatter.
Why can't you treat us fair?
I didn't ask you to love me, I only asked you to care.
Black man dead in Missouri, Staten Island and in Cleveland a child.
We asked why you killed them and all you do is smile.
You took an oath to uphold the law, did it include
killing Black men because you are the boss?
I tell you cops, I don't understand,
Why you fear the Black man?
We bleed red blood, and we cry real tears,
All that we really want is to live.
We demand a change,
things can't remain the same.
No justice, no peace,
Is that right police?

MY PEOPLE

Lord I look around, don't like what I see,
My people seem so lost.
Drinking, drugging, fighting, living in a world of sin.
My Lord, my God when shall it end?
Is there anything that I can do to help?
Lord please show me a way,
Satan appear to be so strong; my people are living so wrong.
Why can't they see,
That all hope lies in Thee.
Today my heart is breaking,
I must answer to your call,
Father I must spread Your gospel,
I must tell it to them all.
I talk to people, but Lord they just don't hear,
If they would just give in, for you are so near.
Lord Your grace is so merciful, and Your love is so good, my
prayer is that someday, my people will do as they should.

NEVER GIVE UP

There are days in my life that I don't want to get up.
I reach for God's word and I read up.
I clasp my hands in prayer and I pray up.
I lift my eyes toward heaven, and I look up.
I open my ears and I listen up.
I close my eyes and surrender all to Christ,
then a smile so bright appears on my face.
For my heart tells me that I can win this race.
How in the world could I have considered giving up?
NEVER, EVER, GIVE UP!!!!!.

LISTEN UP

Listen, slavery time is gone,
Guess what, you better leave me alone.
You are not treating my people right,
It's time that we all see the light.
You treat me anyway that you want to,
when you are in a bind, you expect me to see you through
It really doesn't work like that,
I'm not some ball that you can pull out of a hat.
If I open my mouth, you say that I am trouble,
And you want to get rid of me on the double.
You constantly attempt to kill my self-respect,
So, now my voice is all that I have left.
I'm human, even though you don't think so,
I'm as smart as a whip, this you already know.
Why do you fear me, I don't understand?
After all I am only a Black woman.
I can't let you push me back; I'm moving ahead and that's a fact. Get
used to me being in high places. Just as I am used to your two faces.

THE WORLD WE LIVE IN

We hurry running to and fro,
Life leading us down empty paths.
Hearts filled with sadness,
In a world that no longer seems to care.
A child who has lost his way,
A woman stuck in traffic,
A man who can't find a job,
The world we live in.
Road rage and school killings,
no peace, just unrest.
Suicide and disturbed minds,
Traffic jams on the highway.
Cluttered fields as far as I can see,
the world we live in.

EPISODE TWO

THE MANY FACES OF LOVE

SISTERS

Sisters are forever as long as life lasts,
nothing can come between us, the future, present, nor the past.
Sisters are to love one another through thick and thin
Be there for each other, just good friends..
The bond between sisters should be so strong,
when they are little and even when they are grown.
Nothing matters other than this fact,
Sisters are sisters and that's that.
Sisters should never let any one stand in their way,
Just love one another and always pray.
Material things may come and go,
But a sister's love can only grow.

WHEN YOU CAN'T REACH
THE ONES THAT YOU LOVE

No matter how you beg and plead,
They won't respond to fulfill their needs.
They run the streets day and night,
For them, there is no Christ.
You see their lives being torn apart,
You know that it's because they don't have Christ in their heart.
You ponder their fate and then you wait,
You pray for change before it's too late.
If one more soul through you I could reach,
In my life, there would be so much peace.
It's ironic that the ones you love the most.
will not claim You, my Lord and Savior as their host.
When you have talked and so hard you have tried,
they keep on telling the same old lies.
When in their eyes fear and desperation you see,
And then you wonder oh Lord, how long shall it be?
Today my Dear Lord, my prayer is,
that my brother Ronald to you his life will give.
In my heart I feel him slipping away,
that's why I am so sad today.

A Mother's Day Prayer

Dear Lord, I know that you are listening, because you always are.
Bless each mother Dear Lord whether she is near or far.
Bless each tired, wrinkled and worn hand,
That cooks, cleans and comfort according to your plan.
Bless eyes that are now growing dim,
Dear Lord, please, please bless them.
Mothers work so very hard,
Bless them, oh bless them Dear Lord.
Bless the tears that fall from their eyes,
as they cry for a wayward child.
Bless them Lord as they walk the floors,
Waiting for their child to come through the door.
Bless Mothers Lord for they are precious in your sight,
Bless them Lord, by day and by night..
Mothers deserve the very best,
Bless them Lord and give them rest.
Hold them close Lord to your heart,
For most of them do more than their part,
Bless them Lord as they kneel and pray,
Bless them Lord in every way.
HAPPY MOTHER'S DAY

FRIENDSHIP

Who can you call a friend?
Someone who will stand by you until the end.
Someone who will go that extra mile,
Won't frown but continue to smile.
A friend you can call in the middle of the night,
They will come no matter what the plight.
A friend will never judge or treat you bad,
will stand by your side, no matter how many times you make him mad.
A friend will tell you when you're wrong,
With every hair brain scheme, he will not play along.
He will rejoice with you in your time of joy,
His love for you will take you far.
Be a good friend and you will find,
A good friend will always stand the test of time.
A good friend will not be here today and gone tomorrow,
but will stand by you in your time of sorrow.

A LOVE SONG

Music in the air, love everywhere,
Romantic scenes, nights in the park.
A stroll down a quiet street,
lovers holding hands, smiling at each person that they meet..

A love song, my heart keeps singing,
Every time that I see your face.
Run my fingers through your hair,
As I kiss your tender lips.

I embrace you with such gladness and joy,
With heart and mind in tune.
My heart just skips a beat,
As I sing a love song.

UNCLE

I woke up one morning feeling oh, so sad,
Just couldn't understand why I felt so bad.
The day before had been good,
I felt that I did all that I could.
Something or someone that I loved was hurt,
there was a problem, I just didn't know what.
Suddenly I find out, that you are ill,
Now dear uncle how do you think that made me feel?
Why didn't you tell me that all was not right?
So, that I could join you in prayer to help with the fight.
Love is wonderful, yet prayer is greater,
Glad that I found out sooner than later.
Know that I am here for you,
I'll do anything that you need me to.
In the meantime, dear uncle I will pray,
For, truly there is no other way.
God can mend and He can heal,
In your case, I know that He will..
Keep the faith and be strong,
God will never, ever leave you alone.

LOVE

So many times, I've passed your house,
I wanted to stop and say,
how much I admire and respect you
and your loving way.
For your family so many sacrifices you've made,
to me you are an awesome lady.
So much you give unselfishly,
You possess the character of a woman that all women hope to be.
A wonderful wife and mother I know that you are,
in your children's eyes, you should be a superstar.
Mr. Odell was a blessed man to have you by his side,
I honestly believe that God always has been
and always will be your guide.
For your family, you have given your best,
In my eyes, you have passed the test.
You have so much love and joy in your heart,
You are truly a Black woman who has done more than her part.
Today, I salute and give you my love,
You are truly a gift from God above.
Your stamina and strength have been an inspiration to me,
An example for the whole world to see.

I admire your courage and strength.

"Goodbye Mr. President

A man with integrity and pride,
With a beautiful wife by your side.
The lessons that you taught, more valuable than gold,
You've made history your story will forever be told.
The odds against you were so great,
You remained humble; never did you retaliate.
The day that you took office I will forever remember,
The first Black President, not just a symbol.
You took a stand for all the people,
It was all about business, you were never a glory seeker.
My heart is sad as I watch you leave,
I'm trying to rejoice, because I don't want to grieve.
Goodbye Mr. President, have a great life.
So glad that you came. I wish you and your family the very best,
know that you are the greatest President that we've had yet.

EPISODE THREE

SUFFERING AND PAIN

Two Worlds'

Caught between two worlds,
Am I a boy or am I a girl?
I don't expect you to understand,
Am I a woman, or a man?
These feelings that I have inside,
Why do you always say that I am lying?
You say that I have no rights,
For every little thing, I have to fight.
Did Christ not die for me too?
Can you tell me what I am supposed to do?
I know what I want and how I feel,
Who are you to tell me it's not real?
Am I to hang my head in shame,
Because my lover and I are the same..
I don't know what your wish is for me,
For I am trapped, and I want to be free.
It's never too late,
You can do it.

ROBERT ROBERTSON

I took my eyes off you for a short while,
You closed your eyes and then you smiled.
Someone called and said Robert has taken his wings,
I shook my head and said, oh it's just a dream.
But somehow the dream didn't end,
I opened my eyes, and you were gone my friend.
I know that you are in a better place,
I will forever see your smiling face.
I am so happy that you loved God,
Your leaving has broken so many hearts.
Shontay, the children and your mom,
Your brothers and sister and then some.
Rest in peace my dear friend,
I know that I will see you again.
Please tell God hello for me,
No more pain my friend, you are finally free.

Missing You Mom

Sixteen mother's days have past,
Since I saw your face last.
No kiss or hug, I feel so sad,
I miss you mom; I miss you so bad.
I know that you are in a better place,
Wish that I could give you flowers and wish you Happy Mother's Day.
I give you flowers, but them you can't smell,
From my eyes a tear just fell.
I long to watch you prepare just one more meal,
When you turned your head, a piece of meat I would steal.
Reminiscing about the good old days,
Love you mom, wish that you could have stayed.
I've got it mom, I know what to say,
You were the greatest mom in this world,
I love you, Happy Mother's Day.
Rest in Heaven.

WHY

Why does history repeat itself?
Sadness and pain is all that's left.
Some things I wanted to end,
Has just reared its ugly head again.
I'm so hurt and tired
Don't want to continue to try.
Losing again in the same old way,
What in the hell can I say?
Another kid raised by another man,
I just don't understand.
This one hurts like hell,
We lose again, oh well.

CIERRA

One of the hardest days of my life,
I took you to be put to sleep..
You were so sick, what else could I do?
Know that I will forever love you.
I can't stop the tears,
You were my dog for thirteen years.
I had to let you go,
Because you were hurting so.
It took everything within me to walk away,
I know that I did what was best for you that day.
I put you first, even though it broke my heart.
Now I must begin to heal, as you make a new start.

Goodbye Cierra, Goodbye!!!!!!

RAVEN LYNETTE

I don't know the depth of your pain,
I can only tell you about mine.
I feel as if my heart is going to burst,
As in God, I continue to put my trust.
My heart is so heavy, my tears continue to fall
I don't understand this, I don't understand it at all.
My sweet, beautiful niece with a heart of gold,
I cry out "Dear God, please save her soul."
Raven, Raven, I will forever say your name.
Know that our world without you will never be the same.
Your goofiness and your beautiful smile,
Memories will have to last us for a while.
Your life was taken without a thought,
Pray that someday the perpetrators will be caught.
Did they know that you were loved?
That you were a gift from God above.
Baby girl, our hearts bleed,
They took your life, there was really no need.
God has gained an Angel, sure wish that you could have stayed.
Even though I know that Heaven is a better place.
My dear, sweet 24-year old niece,
Rest on, rest on for God has given you peace.
Auntie Pat loves you, Raven Lynette

DENNIS REMEMBERING MY BROTHER

I remember carrying you on my hip when you were a child,
For any man you would go the extra mile.
Your generosity, your kindness, your smile,
Baby brother, I really love your style..
You gave so much of yourself and everything else
Dennis you loved your family with all of your
heart, just as I loved you from the start..
We were once 4 and now we are 3,
God why did you take him away from me?
I am trying so hard to understand,
I know God that it was part of your master plan.
Dennis do just one thing for me, enjoy your
freedom, for indeed you are free.
Momma came to me the other day, she said
baby everything will be alright.,
Your baby brother is in the arms of Jesus, I am getting ready to bake
him a cake, he is laughing, I won't have to share with anybody else.
This is not goodbye, I will see you again, my baby brother, my friend.
It's hard for me to go on, but I know that God's love will keep me strong.
Love You Brother. Your Sister.... Pat Thomas

WHEN I AM OLD

When I am old, I hope to be,
Full of life and fancy free.
Have kind thoughts and a clear mind,
With vivid memories of things left behind.
I don't want to be mean and hate the world,
I want to be loved by little boys and girls.
I want to be able to understand,
The young, the old and my fellow man.
I want to be able to reminisce,
About when I was young and my first kiss.
I want to be able to laugh and to love,
I want my soul to be as free as a dove.
When I am Old.

LOST

We've lost Magic Johnson to aids,
Lynn Bias to the grave.
Dexter Manley to cocaine,
Can you tell me brothers, just why all the pain?
A good living each of you had the ability to make,
Yet, like fools you rushed in forgetting what was at stake.
You had a chance to set examples,
Instead you chose wild sex and drugs to sample.
My heart cries out because I don't understand,
God gave each of you a gift, put destiny in your hands.
For some reason or the other,
You chose the path of destruction my Black brothers.
Lost in a world, where there is so much to gain,
Creating chaos, blocking the sunshine, bringing forth the rain.
Someday my brothers, I hope that you will see,
We don't need wild sex or drugs, for God has already made us free.
Shame is what I feel deep inside,
The disappointment makes me want to run and hide.
I continue to believe and pray,
Knowing that God will fix it someday.

EPISODE FOUR

ALL ABOUT GOD

MAN, OF GOD

With clarity and conviction, you speak the word of God,
Not your thoughts, yet they come from the heart.
Plain and simple, the instructions that you give,
Showing the world how to forever live.
The story of Naaman, Joseph and Noah too,
A person, a place and instructions on what to do.
The blueprint step by step,
Showing man, glory be to God, how to help himself.
The words that you speak, a child can understand,
Salvation for every woman,, boy, girl and man.
I am excited and my strength is renewed,
Thanks so much for your knowledge, wisdom and spiritual food.
I am so glad that you came,
Always and forever, proclaim God's name. The Church of Christ,
the one that He built, will forever stand and never wilt.

GOD'S PEACE

There are no words that I can say,
That will make your pain go away.
I don't even know how you feel,
For He gave His son's life so that we might live.
Look to Him for perfect peace,
In time, He shall give you relief.
I know that your heart is sad,
Being human at times you even get mad.
Look to Jesus for He holds the key,
He will give you perfect peace.
You have been through so much,
Just keep holding on to God and in Him put all your trust.
Someday perfect peace will surely come,
Just as sure as the rising of the sun.

THE WORLD TODAY

Visiting the zoo, having fun,
When out of nowhere the terror begun.
Gun shots ringing out,
Children scrambling all about.
Our Father who art in heaven is all that I can say,
The world that we live in is in such a sad state.
Innocent children, no longer safe,
God is there no hiding place?
Children hurt and parents upset,
A feeling of lost and total regret.
A child lying brain dead,
With a gunshot wound to the head.
My heart aches and I don't understand,
What is to happen to the soul of man?
I pray for change, it truly must come,
On this earth may God's will be done..
We must join together and pray,
People there is no other way. Our children's lives are
at stake, we must pray now, before it's too late.

LET GOD BE MY JUDGE

We come to church, sing and pray,
Commune, give and go our way.
Sometimes we whisper about a sister across the aisle,
Or say something negative about a hollering child.
Where is the Spirit, where can it be?
We don't have any of that love that God has shown for you and me.
When will we stop trying to judge one another?
Come together and love like real sisters and brothers.
Each of you, turn around and look at yourself,
Before you decide that for me there is no help.
Let me be judged by God above,
For He doesn't get high and He doesn't do drugs.
So, hey man leave the judging alone,
Mind your business and I'll take care of my own.
When the day comes, God will judge the right from the wrong.
God will be totally fair,
I won't be judged by the color of my hair.
I won't be sent to hell because of the mood He's in,
Or simply because I'm not His best friend.
Can you imagine God saying, I saw you drunk last night?
You started a fight, you can't make it to heaven, you're just not right.
That sounds more or less like you and me,
Not my Savior, the One who died to set us free.
Let us do that which we can, that is to love and respect our fellow man.
Don't worry about the liar, the drunk or me,
Let God be my judge, not Thomas Lee.
Put the Spirit back in the church where it belongs,
Show love, joy, peace, long suffering, gentleness,
goodness and faith, and start your journey home.

HAPPY BIRTHDAY...
HAPPY TIMES,

HAPPY BIRTHDAY BROTHER

Dear brother, I love you with all of my heart,
You are very special to me.
I hope that this day is filled with love and joy for you.
If I had one wish for you, it would be,
That your heart and soul are free.
I could wish for you silver and gold, but it would soon decay,
So I wish for you instead God's love,
For it will never fade away.
The things that I wish for you are simple, they don't cost a dime,

I simply want you to have LOVE, JOY and PEACE of mind.
Today and every day, please know,
That I love you, but God loves you more.
I wish for you, many more years to come,
I am so glad that you know Jesus
God's only son.

HAPPY FATHER'S DAY

You are the father of my children, the lover of my life,
This day and every day I'm glad to be your wife.
You are a wonderful father, so loving and kind,
God has given you strength, good will and a determined mind.
With the kids when they were small,
You gave them everything, you gave them your ALL.
There are times sweetheart when you are as silly as a child,
For your family you have always gone that extra mile.
As I look back over the years,
My eyes begin to feel with tears,
I see you there sharing your love,
There is no doubt in my mind,
you are the greatest father in this world.
You've made my life wonderful and grand,
You're not only a good father, you're also a good man.
You are a father with courage and dedication too, on this
special day, we wish A HAPPY FATHER'S DAY TO YOU.

Eighteen Years

I remember the day that you were born,
Your dad holding you in his arms.
You were so tiny and small,
Yet, you have been the greatest gift of all.
I thank God for your life each and every day,
For your wellbeing I always pray.
I ask God to guide and keep you safe,
To keep you healthy and full of grace.
I love your spirit and your smile,
So glad that you are my grandchild.
So much joy you have brought to my life,
You are not only beautiful, but you are also nice.
On this your eighteenth birthday,
My darling grandchild I would like to say,
I love you more than life itself,
I love you to life and not to death.

HAPPY BIRTHDAY

I remember the day that you were born,
My sister was one proud mom.
You were pretty and pink like a rose,
It has been such a blessing watching your life unfold.
Your life has not been perfect; you've always done your
best, what you couldn't do, you trusted God to do the
rest. Your smile is infectious, your generosity amazing.
You work extremely hard; you have never been lazy.
As you approach a different phase of your life, keep walking,
walking with Christ. The road ahead for you is paved with
gold, unfinished business so many stories to be told.
Today God has blessed you with FORTY years, surrounded by family
and friends; to each of them you are so dear. Enjoy this day: keep that
beautiful smile on your face. With all of my heart, my darling niece.
I wish you a Happy Birthday!!!
LOVE YOU

"50 YEARS"

My, where did the time go,
You were just a little girl
Or at least I thought so.
The cutest kid with a crooked smile,
You were such a beautiful child.
You were mischievous, yet smart,
I love you with all my heart.
You have so much dignity and pride,
A whole lot of love inside.
I am so thankful to God for your life,
For He spared it not once but twice.
I pray that God grants you a hundred years more,
That your spirit will remain high and that you will always soar.
50 years my little girl,
To me you mean the world.
Love you, Happy Birthday,
Go on and have your way.
Love, Mom

NINETY-NINE YEARS

Dear God thank you so much for the life of this man right here,
To me, he is so precious and dear.
I love him more than I could ever explain.
I call him uncle Buddy, but Alex is his name.
He is handsome, witty and kool,
For him I would break every rule.
A man with integrity and heart,
I've loved him from the very start.
99 years, what a blessing, I see the smile on your face.
I hear your laughter, that resonates in this place,
I love you with everything within me.
Happy, Happy Birthday!!!!

60TH BIRTHDAY

Today you have reached a milestone,
proof that God has never left you alone.
He has blessed you in a mighty way,
To live, to see another birthday.
He has smiled upon you with His grace and love,
Took care of you, even when you were a little girl.
Linda, God has given you beauty and a great smile,
Strength to run that extra mile.
You are my sister, don't ever forget,
One of the sweetest people that I have met.
I wish for you a hundred years more,
For you I know that God has great things in store.
Embrace this day with open arms,
You're getting older, no need for alarm.
Today I wish for you nothing but the best,
I love you sister, God bless.

EIGHT YEARS

I remember it, as if it was yesterday,
In your mom's arms you did lay.
You were so little and pretty,
I knew even then that you would be silly.
Watching you grow down through the years,
Sometimes to my eyes it brings tears

You are beautiful and so very smart,
I love you with all my heart.
Eight years that's how old that you are today,
Wish that I could be there, so that we could play.
So, glad God allowed me to be your great grandmother,
Because I love you like no other.
Go on and enjoy your ice cream and cake,
Always remember, never be fake.
HAPPY BIRTHDAY LITTLE GIRL!!!!!!
You will always be a part of my world.

STRUGGLES

The children's march, my time in jail, oh Martin I have a story to tell.
But today is all about you,
The words that you spoke and how you brought us through.
Freedom, liberty and justice for all,
How you remained nonviolent,
Even when your back was against the wall.
You wanted for us, what we should have already had.
The way you were treated was oh, so sad,
You will forever remain in the hearts of men,
Thank you for your gift to defend.
For the cause you gave your life,
Leaving behind your children and wife.
I love you Dr. King
HAPPY BIRTHDAY

Episode Six

Miscellaneous

THE BEAUTY THAT GOD CREATED

The vast beauty of the sky,
Mountains rising high.
Serene, as peaceful as can be,
Leaves blowing on the trees, they are so free.
A calmness that I can't explain,
A beauty that has no name.
So inviting, so real,
If you only knew how it makes me feel.
Only God can get the credit for this,
Man can not claim it no matter how hard he may wish.
Astounding beauty that takes your breath away,
Leaves you speechless with no words to say.
I could sit here and watch for hours,
The sky, the trees and the flowers.
Thank God for the beauty that He created,
It is so marvelous, just as I have stated.

NOTHING IS THE SAME

With mom and dad gone and all the rest,
Nothing seems the same, I just do my best.
Birthdays, holidays most of the spark is gone,
At times I feel so all alone.
I know they wouldn't want me to feel this way,
It's a feeling that I really don't want to stay.
I'm thankful for good memories, I really am,
Still at times I want to shake my head and just say damn.
This thing called life, I really don't understand,
I know that it is all a part of God's master plan.
I see beauty in the blue skies,
Yet, there are tears in my eyes.
Missing love ones and friends,
Dreams appear to be coming to an end.
Feeling a little helpless right now,
But with God I know that I will make it somehow.
Pray for me.

HATE

How can you sit there with a smile on your face,
Say that you hate me because of my race.
T he same God that created you,
Is the One who made me too.
I'm His child and I know this to be the truth,
You can't destroy me, no matter what you do.
You might as well face it, Blacks are here to stay,
God meant for it to be that way.
He didn't say that you were right because you're white,
He did say that we are all precious in His sight.
Fill your heart with love and not color,
Then you will be able to accept your Black sisters and brothers.
To hate puts you in danger of hell fire,
I'm sure that hell is not the place that you desire.
Fix it before it's to late,
Remember that only love can conquer hate.

A SAD AMERICA

In my life I have never seen,
People be so divisive and mean
Trouble in every place that you look,
Even want to make Trump president, when clearly he's a crook.
Common decency in this world no longer has a place,
People still being judged by their race.
Black people continue to kill one another,
Not realizing that we are all sisters and brothers.
The media has gone wild, distort everything they touch,
Doesn't matter if it's a lie as long as they keep the ratings up.
Facts are fantasy, they don't care,
Love their fellow man, they wouldn't dare.
I know for sure that God is in charge,
So, I will take none of this foolishness to heart.
No matter who leads the country or what's going on,
My faith in God will remain strong.
All of my faith and hope I put in Him,
That's why I don't worry about them.
Everything is going to be alright,
No matter if the world turns upside down, God will win the fight.

THAT DAY

The day started just like any other,
Before it ended the world was in trouble.
In all of my life I would have never dreamed,
Of the devastation and ruin that I have seen.
September 11, 2001 will be a day that we can't forget,
The sadness and frustration in our hearts will always be kept,
The tears that we've shed and the lives that were lost,
Oh my God, it was all without a cause.
How can, how can this be?
We live in America, land of the brave and home of the free.
I close my eyes, yet sleep won't come,
All that I can see is mothers and fathers that will never go home.
For the love of God my prayer is,
That this nightmare will soon end.
This tragedy affects each of us,
Oh Lord, in thee we must put our trust.
To the family of victims hurt or lost,
My heart moans for you.
Tomorrow this thing could happen to me,
For we don't know where the end is you see.
We as a nation must kneel and pray,
Please God we need a healing today.
Will we ever again feel safe and free?
I don't know we must wait and see.

FOR EVERYTHING THERE IS A REASON

I close my eyes and guess what I see,
That sweet smile of Blackness all around me.
He had a sense of humor that was so unique,
To me the man was so sweet.
He was loved and well known,
Because of that you will never walk alone.
God gave you a wonderful soul mate,
You will surely see him again someday.
Our paths only crossed for a brief while,
But I could tell that he had class and a lot of style.
Sometimes my job is so very hard,
Especially when I forget to let go and let God.
Life is funny sometimes, but God is the key
and He will give you peace of mind.
My prayer for you is,
You will get past his death and continue to live.
May God bless and keep you.

SPECIAL CARE

Get in that tub and out real quick,
Let me tell you sweetie, I'm no young chick.
My hair is gray, my teeth are few,
I'm doing the best that I can do.
Please don't rush me, let me take my time,
After all I am only 89.
Age has made me wrinkled and slow,
But I am still a human being, don't you know?
My hands may fumble the button a time or two,
I know it may seem as if I'll never get through.
Bear with me, if you please,
I'm just old it's not a disease.
When I say I don't want my meds before my meal,
Don't get upset it's no big deal.
Humor me in my old age,
After all I am old enough to set the stage.
Special care you should be able to work, don't pull, rush or jerk.
Speak slowly so that I may understand, remember
that I am here because I need a helping hand.

THE LONG RACE AGAINST DIABETES

Hold on, hold out fight, fight, fight.
Run the race with all your might.
When you're being pricked and stuck,
Hold your head up high, don't give up.
Stand tall with your head erect,
Make diabetes give you respect.
Go to diabetic teaching class, learn about nutrition,
Learn the facts, forget about the fiction.
Run the race with knowledge and zeal,
Don't be controlled by needles or pills.
Your legs are long, rise above,
Conquer this thing with God's grace and love.
Be receptive, let your mind be your guide,
Keep your eyes checked, so that your vision won't subside.
Take control, learn all that you can, diabetes is
only a disease-this you must understand.
It's a long, long race, you can do it, devise a plan and stick to it.

ROOM 24

When I walked into his room that day,
I cried out oh God, I just can't stay.
A small voice inside my head,
Said close your eyes and pray.
Dear God is what I said, please help me to endure,
Make this awful smell go away or tone it down for sure.
This man needs what I have to give, so please
dear God let it be thou will.
Let me be able to stand this test,
Allow me to give this man my best.
I am not going to tell you that the smell went completely away,
However, God fixed it, so that I could stay.
He is such an awesome God, so worthy to be praised,
Putting me where I needed to be and allowing me to stay.
I thank God for allowing me to serve, for helping me give
room 24 all the care and love that he deserved.

LOSS

To lose someone that's still alive,
A pain that hurts deep inside.
They are walking this earth, yet in your life they play no part,
Dear God please protect my heart.
I am hurting deep within,
Someday this pain and frustration must end.
I love, that's all I know how to do,
Never thought that I would lose you.
I'll pray for you every single day,
My prayer is that you find your way.
You must feel so empty and lost,
Hope that someday, you will explore the cause.
I've decided to walk away,
Know that I will be here if you decide to come back some day.
I'll love you from afar,
And forever wish upon a star.

TAXI

Hands up!
Taxi, I need a ride...you know the yellow thing
with 4 tires and the sign on top,
Taxi, taxi please stop.
Be careful what you wish for, it could end your hopes and dreams.
Taxi, taxi so innocent it seems
Rolling down the street letting people inside,
Why because they need a ride,
The yellow thing with 4 tires and the sign on top.
Take me to my destination, here is the address,
Wait, wait where am I,
Not a house, not a person around,
Not even a sound.
What are you doing, get off me.
Taxi, taxi the yellow thing with 4 tires and
the sign on top please, please stop
As my rights are violated and my pride is taken, as you
squeeze inside my body and the heavens disappear,
my heart, my heart has been ripped apart.
Taxi, taxi that yellow thing with 4 tires and the sign, the sign on top.
Taxi

WHY DO YOU STAY

Guess what, I look at you my eyes fill with tears,
I see your pain, I see your fears.
You've been called every name under the sun,
You're no good, you're not a good father...
You don't even work, you don't even know how to fuck.
You're worthless, just a piece of shit, why do you stay?
You've done all that you could to make her life
better, yet she throws you to the wolves,
Questions your manhood.
Your mind is in orbit, your feet never touch the ground,
damn she treats you like dirt, why do you stay?
Your mind is racing, your heart is broken, your
spirit is so lost, floating through the air,
Damn I wish that she would care.
All she does is criticize, please escape, run before it's to late.
She calls you messy and weak, now that's not the you that I see.
I ask again, why do you stay?
The violence that she inflicts upon you, as she punches you in the face,
The constant reminder that you are a disgrace.
You are surrounded by insanity, I beg you please
break free, duck, hide save yourself.
You can do it, I know you can, because after all you are
a man, even though she says that you are not.,
Damn her and every word that comes out of her mouth.
Why do you stay?

A MISUNDERSTANDING

The harsh words that came from your lips,
Don't think that I'll ever forget.
Your words have left me in a state of confusion,
Did it really happen or was it an illusion?
I close my eyes, it feels like a nightmare,
I can't believe that you really don't care.
Something inside of you must really be broken,
We are your family and not just a token.
I pray God's forgiveness for you,
For only He can see you through.
There is a weariness deep in my soul,
Sadness that I can't control.
Even though the sun is shining bright,
I see darkness not a glimmer of light.
A broken heart, tear filled eyes,
Emptiness, no warmth inside.

I Don't Understand

Why so much pain?
Can anyone explain?
Why the tears in my eyes?
Why do I feel so tired?
I just can't fight any more,
How will this story end though?
I feel as if I want to scream,
Why can't I wake up from this nightmare or is it just a dream?
To love sometime requires to much, who wins in this search?
I have really given my all,
Still I've lost.
I don't feel like bouncing back,
Now that I have fallen off the track.
I must pray because I don't understand,
I'm so damn angry man.

SUICIDE

I don't know what you are thinking,
I don't know your level of despair.
True life is not fair.
Always know there is someone who cares.
Dark and sleepless nights,
The struggle is real always a fight.
Death is permanent there is no return,
Once you do it, it's really done.
I have dark days too,
Times that I don't know what to do.
I never want to hurt myself,
Nor do I want to hurt anyone else.
Death is not your only way out,
Don't let your woes or troubles cause you to doubt.
Suicide is not the way,
What else can I say?

HIDDEN FEELINGS

We walk around and we pretend,
I love you, I'm your friend.
When all the bullshit is stuck inside,
Makes me angry and the truth I can no longer hide.
You keep holding on to the past,
Bad memories shouldn't really last.
You blame someone else for everything that was done,
Cruel conversations, you're really no fun.
When you speak all that I hear is anger,
Living on the edge puts your heart in danger.
Do you really truly love?
As God has commanded from above.
Maybe someday you can heal,
If not your world will forever stand still.
Hidden feelings, unspoken words,
Hang on to that hate but know that it's absurd.

Why Raven

The pain in my heart won't stop,
Your life ended with the tick of the clock.
That low life led you to your death,
There was no way that you could have gotten help.
The shock you must have felt as he fired the gun,
Striking you in your heart and lung.
Damn I feel the pain,
God knows that dude must have been insane.
Why I will never understand,
Tell me why did you have to kill her man?
She was beautiful and smart,
I'm asking you why Dear God?
Raven your smile was as bright as the morning sun,
Your work down here is done.
We will meet again someday,
In that land so far away.
Auntie loves you.

HAPPY BIRTHDAY

Happy birthday in heaven doesn't sound right,
Dennis I have cried all night.
Want to call and ask, did you get your card?
Man, this is so hard.
I hear your voice; I see your face.
Really missing you from this place.
I know momma baked you a cake,
Don't eat it all, it will make your stomachache.
Happy Birthday brother is all that I can say,
I love you; this will always be your day.

YOU MADE ME HATE YOU

You made me hate you because of who you are,
I tried to love you, I tried with all of my heart.
The more you hurt me the harder I tried,
Now there is nothing, I feel nothing inside.
I tried to give you encouragement, showed you love,
What I got in return was deceit and empty words.
I've cried into my pillow so many nights,
Asking God to please make it right.
Each day you drift farther into your own space,
God knows it's not a happy place.
I did all that I could to make your life better,
I'm just to weak now, those storms I can no longer weather.
I'll continue to pray for you, after all that's what I do,
I tried so hard not to hate you.
You've destroyed something so important to me,
I'm in danger of losing my soul, for hate is not
allowed, only love. God help me.

A Prayer At Jordan Hare

A miracle some may say,
You know Auburn came to play.
Everyone said they didn't stand a chance,
Hold my mule and watch me dance.
Up and down the field they went,
I saw an Angel sitting on the fence.
When things really started to look bad,
I bowed my head, and this is what I said.
God football I know you don't play,
Just take a listen as I pray.
This game we really need to win,
Dropped my head and said AMEN!
43 seconds left to go,
100 yards to make the score.
Number 11, Chris Davis RUN,
Auburn, job well done.
34-28
Can you say great?
WAR EAGLE